ISBN 979-8-218-45111-0
Ingram Spark

TAP INTO GOD'S TRUTH

The Bible stands apart from any other literary work—it consists of an entire collection of books, each written by a diverse group of people, spanning centuries. What makes the Bible truly extraordinary is that its varied human writers found inspiration from a singular divine author—God himself. When referring to the scriptures, the apostle Paul uses the term "inspired by God," which translates to "God-breathed" in Greek. That means the words of the Bible possess the potential to effect profound change and transformation in our lives. Paul goes on to help us understand that all of Scripture is "inspired by God and is profitable for teaching, for rebuking, for correcting, for training in righteousness."

In our attempt to understand who God is, discern His purposes, and grasp His truths for our lives, neglecting the Bible is not an option. In a very real sense, the Bible serves as the "instruction manual" for life. The Creator of our existence has outlined standards, plans, and purposes for us within its pages. Without studying the contents of this "instruction manual", we remain oblivious to His intentions and lack the guidance to live according to His design.

Unfortunately, many individuals don't give much effort in exploring the depths of the Bible. Sometimes, this stems from laziness or misplaced priorities, or just struggling to understand the text they are reading. Its true, the Bible can prove challenging to understand at times. And while its foundational teachings can be understood by children, numerous aspects within its pages demand additional effort and guidance.

If you want to get the most out of the Bible, you need to learn how to read and interpret it for yourself.

We hope this journal will help you do just that. This journal was created to help you get the most out of your biblical reading and study as you tap into the eternal truths God reveals to us throughout Scripture. And to help you create a plan and habit of reading the Bible on a regular basis.

KEYS FOR YOUR READING

Using the acronym **TAP**, we have created key sections in this journal to help you tap into God's truth.

Truth

In our exploration of the Bible, it's crucial to stay attuned to the main themes and essential teachings, while avoiding getting too sidetracked by secondary matters. It's like peering through a telescope to see the big picture before delving into the details with a microscope. The Bible isn't a riddle book or a coded message, so there's no need to search for intricate symbols and hidden meanings. Instead, focus on what it meant to the original readers and how those insights apply to your life today. In doing so, you unveil the timeless truths that God desires for us to grasp.

As you write in this section each day, write down the eternal truth(s) that the Holy Spirit is revealing to you from your reading.

Application

The ultimate goal of reading and studying the Bible is not to showcase theological expertise or engage in intellectual debates, but rather to apply its teachings to our everyday lives. Bible study is not about impressing others; it's about allowing God's Word to bring about a transformative impact. So, as you read the Bible, listen to the Holy Spirit attentively—and then respond with obedience. With that in mind, as we read the Scriptures, we should do it with humility and an open heart, prepared to be both challenged and changed by God's truths. An open-minded attitude is key. Let go of preconceptions, assumptions, and prior knowledge. Embrace the potential for fresh revelations each time you engage with the Bible. Its pages are a wellspring of inexhaustible truths.

As you write in this section, write down how you will obey God's eternal truth(s) and apply His word to your life.

Prayer

The Bible is a book filled with spiritual wisdom and diving into it requires a spiritual mindset. You engage in studying the Bible spiritually when your reading is partnered with prayer. This approach allows the Holy Spirit to shed light on the understanding and application of its truths in your life. So, let your reading and study be wrapped in prayer. This will let the Holy Spirit guide your exploration of the profound insights within the pages of the Bible.

And as you write in this section, write a prayer asking God to help you to live out the eternal truth you have read about.

Sabbath Days

The Sabbath is a weekly oasis in the hustle and bustle of life. It's a day set apart for rest, reflection, and connection—with both God and others. Imagine it as a divine reset button, reminding us to pause, recharge, and recalibrate our focus on what truly matters. In the rhythm of our fast-paced lives, the Sabbath acts as a steady heartbeat, offering a space for spiritual rejuvenation. It's not just a break from work but a sacred invitation to experience the richness of God's presence and delve into the truths embedded in His Word. Observing the Sabbath isn't a legalistic duty; it's a relational embrace, an intentional choice to honor God's design for our well-being and find a sanctuary of peace amidst life's demands. Embracing the Sabbath means recognizing that we're not just called to be doers but also to be dwellers in the rest God provides, ensuring our souls are nourished, inspired, and ready to obey Him in the week ahead.

On these days, reflect on the past week and write down what God has taught you and how thankful you are for it.

OVERVIEW - JOEL

There is much ambiguity concerning the prophet Joel. He is sent to
the people of Judah and like just about every other prophet in the Old
Testament, his words are a warning to the people of God. They have turned
away from the LORD with a message to repent, and the hope of blessing
from Him.

The locusts will come and devour crops leaving nothing behind. Sons and
daughters will be sold as slaves. The people must decide whether they
will serve the LORD or not as the day of the LORD's reckoning is quickly
approaching. May God's people humble themselves and seek His face. As we
read Joel, may we be reminded that the LORD's punishment is real and fierce
however, He is king and forgiving.

DAY 1

JOEL 1:1-12

Context

The prophet Joel recounts the plague that decimated their lands, a layered attack from the palmerworm, locust, cankerworm, and caterpillar. Each wave of warriors destroyed increasingly more of the land until there was nothing left. So the prophet calls on the drunkards to weep and the inhabitants of Judah to mourn in sackcloth like a virgin grieving for her husband.

TRUTH: What is the eternal truth that God is revealing to you?

____

____

____

____

____

APPLICATION: How will you apply this truth to your life?

____

____

____

____

____

PRAYER: Ask God to help you to live out this truth.

____

____

____

____

____

DAY 2

JOEL 1:13-20

Context

Joel calls for the leadership of Israel to mourn in sackcloth and lead the people into a time of fasting with the hope that the Lord will show them his mercy. He describes the coming devastation and how it will spare no living thing. The streams will dry up and the trees will burn, causing the wildlife to groan in despair.

TRUTH: What is the eternal truth that God is revealing to you?

____

____

____

____

____

APPLICATION: How will you apply this truth to your life?

____

____

____

____

____

PRAYER: Ask God to help you to live out this truth.

____

____

____

____

____

DAY 3

JOEL 2:1-17

Context

The day of the Lord is coming, a day of judgment, darkness, and devastation like the people have never known. God invites his people to repent, not repentance full of outward piety like tearing garments, but rent hearts and brokenness.

TRUTH: What is the eternal truth that God is revealing to you?

____

____

____

____

____

APPLICATION: How will you apply this truth to your life?

____

____

____

____

____

PRAYER: Ask God to help you to live out this truth.

____

____

____

____

____

DAY 4
JOEL 2:18-32

Context

God assures them that a true heartfelt repentance will restore them to prosperity and safety, never again experiencing shame from other nations. This chapter ends with a promise, that one day, God will pour out his spirit on all flesh and that anyone who calls on him will be saved.

TRUTH: What is the eternal truth that God is revealing to you?

____

____

____

____

____

APPLICATION: How will you apply this truth to your life?

____

____

____

____

PRAYER: Ask God to help you to live out this truth.

____

____

____

____

DAY 5

JOEL 3

Context

The book of Joel ends with the Lord promising to enact judgment on all nations that have been hostile towards his chosen people, nations like the Phoenicians and Philistines will not go unpunished for their hostility. He calls them to prepare for war, to beat their plows into swords and pruning hooks into spears declaring that The Day of the Lord is soon to come. He ends with their glorious future and a land free from the foreign powers.

TRUTH: What is the eternal truth that God is revealing to you?

____

____

____

____

____

APPLICATION: How will you apply this truth to your life?

____

____

____

____

____

PRAYER: Ask God to help you to live out this truth.

____

____

____

____

____

OVERVIEW - AMOS

Unlike many of the prophets we read of in scripture, Amos was a shepherd from Tekoa and not the son of a prophet or priest. He was given a vision from the LORD to give to God's people and moved in swift obedience to the instructions given to him.

Amos's mission was to confront the children of Israel who strayed from their faithfulness to the Lord's ways. In their time of peace from war and abundance, Israel began to partake in oppressing the poor by selling them into slavery. They also grew complacent in their relationship with the Father, forsaking faith in exchange for religious traditions. This book is a message of judgment to God's people with a warning of the impending circumstances they would face for their disobedience.

DAY 6
AMOS 1

Context

In the first chapter of Amos the prophet powerfully declares that Yahweh will not turn a blind eye to anyone's blatant sin, even if the culprit is his chosen people. The tearful prayers of the oppressed and hurting are heard by the ancient of days and will not go unanswered. This chapter serves as a powerful reminder for us to uphold the banner of justice while shunning cruelty and living righteously, for God refuses to be impartial with his judgments and His mercy is with those who do good.

TRUTH: What is the eternal truth that God is revealing to you?

____

____

____

____

____

APPLICATION: How will you apply this truth to your life?

____

____

____

____

____

PRAYER: Ask God to help you to live out this truth.

____

____

____

____

____

DAY 7

Sabbath Day

Today marks a Rest Day. The focus is simple: rest in the presence of God. Whether it's an opportunity to catch up on the reading plan, journal reflections on your spiritual journey, or engage in concentrated prayer, the key is to spend meaningful time in God's presence. Take this day to reconnect, absorb the lessons learned, and prioritize a moment of restful communion with God.

Reflect and write about what God has taught you this past week.

DAY 8

AMOS 2

Context

In this chapter, the author paints a vivid picture of the results that come when we migrate from the commandments of God, deal treacherously with our neighbor, and wallow in the filth of sin. Yet, his unfailing love is ever shining and drawing us to himself even in the darkness that's domiciled in our hearts. Like a loving father doesn't aim to harm his children when he disciplines them, the goal of the father's chastisement here is not utter annihilation, but repentance.

TRUTH: What is the eternal truth that God is revealing to you?

____

____

____

____

____

APPLICATION: How will you apply this truth to your life?

____

____

____

____

____

PRAYER: Ask God to help you to live out this truth.

____

____

____

____

____

DAY 9

AMOS 3

Context

Amos 3 shows us that those who have been chosen by God bear a heavy responsibility to align themselves with his commandments. The people refused to obey the word of God and heed the many warnings of his prophets heaping on themselves divine judgment as God continued to prove himself to be a God of justice and righteousness.

TRUTH: What is the eternal truth that God is revealing to you?

____

____

____

____

____

APPLICATION: How will you apply this truth to your life?

____

____

____

____

____

PRAYER: Ask God to help you to live out this truth.

____

____

____

____

____

DAY 10

AMOS 4

Context

In Chapter 4 we see the results of continued rebellion and the necessity of repentance. As God continues to use many different means of correction, this rod is one of love. The Father desires that we have a sincere devotion to him, not just mere platitudes and going through the motions. A relationship that yields the fruit of a radically transformed inward life that pours out to the oppressed and marginalized.

TRUTH: What is the eternal truth that God is revealing to you?

____

____

____

____

____

APPLICATION: How will you apply this truth to your life?

____

____

____

____

____

PRAYER: Ask God to help you to live out this truth.

____

____

____

____

____

____

DAY 11
AMOS 5:1-17

Context

Amos 1 opens with a cry of the coming demise due to Israel's continued rebellion. But God, still rich in mercy will allow only a remnant to remain. The prophet pleads with the people to repent and turn away from worthless idols and their cruel treatment of the needy and oppressed, urging them to uphold God's commandments of justice and righteousness.

TRUTH: What is the eternal truth that God is revealing to you?

____

____

____

____

____

APPLICATION: How will you apply this truth to your life?

____

____

____

____

____

PRAYER: Ask God to help you to live out this truth.

____

____

____

____

____

DAY 12

AMOS 5:18-27

Context

The people are deceived into believing that the day of the Lord is one of rejoicing and blessing, Amos warns them that their interpretation is flawed and that they will be judged for their unrepentant sinfulness. The prophet passionatley scolds them for their meaningless rituals, idolatrous worship, and injustice to the oppressed, concluding this chapter with a morbid prophecy about the fate of the unrepentant Israelites.

TRUTH: What is the eternal truth that God is revealing to you?

____

____

____

____

____

APPLICATION: How will you apply this truth to your life?

____

____

____

____

____

PRAYER: Ask God to help you to live out this truth.

____

____

____

____

____

DAY 13

AMOS 6

Context

In Chapter 6 it is those who are at ease in Zion with their beds of ivory, comfortable couches, and the best food and wine that will be the first to drink from the bitter cup of God's judgment. This chapter shows how God harshly judges those who live in opulence and refuse to lend a hand to the suffering. As believers, we must keep our hearts soft to the needs of others and not be distracted by materialistic pleasures or self-glorification.

TRUTH: What is the eternal truth that God is revealing to you?

______

______

______

______

______

APPLICATION: How will you apply this truth to your life?

______

______

______

______

______

PRAYER: Ask God to help you to live out this truth.

______

______

______

______

______

DAY 14

Sabbath Day

Today marks a Rest Day. The focus is simple: rest in the presence of God. Whether it's an opportunity to catch up on the reading plan, journal reflections on your spiritual journey, or engage in concentrated prayer, the key is to spend meaningful time in God's presence. Take this day to reconnect, absorb the lessons learned, and prioritize a moment of restful communion with God.

Reflect and write about what God has taught you this past week.

DAY 15

AMOS 7

Context

In Chapter 7 the shepherd-turned prophet Amos is willing to stand boldly and declare the judgment of the Lord regardless of the opposition from powerful religious figures. Though his words are very strong and confrontational he still stands as an intercessor for his people showing not only courage but deep compassion for his fellow countrymen.

TRUTH: What is the eternal truth that God is revealing to you?

____

____

____

____

____

APPLICATION: How will you apply this truth to your life?

____

____

____

____

____

PRAYER: Ask God to help you to live out this truth.

____

____

____

____

____

DAY 16
AMOS 8

Context

As this book comes to its climax the prophet sees a vision of a basket of summer fruit, a terrifying symbol that the time is ripe for Israel's judgment. Detailed descriptions of death, calamity, and mourning fill the page as those who exploited the suffering and needy receive their just rewards. The most devastating of all isn't the carnage or the famine of bread and water but of God's silence, for they will yearn to hear a word from him to no avail.

TRUTH: What is the eternal truth that God is revealing to you?

____

____

____

____

____

APPLICATION: How will you apply this truth to your life?

____

____

____

____

____

PRAYER: Ask God to help you to live out this truth.

____

____

____

____

____

DAY 17

AMOS 9

Context

The final chapter of the book of Amos is the most powerful and encouraging portion of the prophet's message. Though this chapter starts with bleak images of God's inescapable judgment it concludes with a promise to restore the fallen house of David and speaks of a promising future where the people of God will never again be uprooted from their land.

TRUTH: What is the eternal truth that God is revealing to you?

APPLICATION: How will you apply this truth to your life?

PRAYER: Ask God to help you to live out this truth.

OVERVIEW - MICAH

Micah served as a prophet to Judah from 742-687 BC. Following King Ahaz's evil reign as he set idols in the temple and closed the doors, King Hezekiah comes in yielding to much of Micah's wisdom. And while the king's honor postpones the judgment that is to fall on the people, their sin eventually leads them into bondage.

The message of Micah to the people of Samaria and Judah is a warning of God's judgment against sin. Their struggles with theft, greed, heresy, injustice, oppression, murder, and more are stirring up the LORD's hate (for sin). And while the LORD is angered by their ungodly behaviors, He is willing to forgive them and restore them as a just judge. What God desires most from this people is their obedience to Him in loving others and operating with justice.

DAY 18
MICAH 1

Context

Chapter 1 of the book of Micah opens with the prophet receiving an ominous revelation of judgment coming upon the nations of Samaria and Jerusalem. His graphic and prophetic imagery of God descending from the heavens and melting the mountains beneath him symbolizes his inescapable judgment for persistent disobedience.

TRUTH: What is the eternal truth that God is revealing to you?

____

____

____

____

____

APPLICATION: How will you apply this truth to your life?

____

____

____

____

____

PRAYER: Ask God to help you to live out this truth.

____

____

____

____

____

____

DAY 19
MICAH 2

Context

In Chapter 2 God addresses the affluent who through manipulation and deception exploit the unexpecting to seize their property. The Lord promises to construct an unavoidable disaster that ends with their land being snatched away from them, receiving no portion of what has been divided. Micah implores the people to shut their ears to the false prophets of their day and pursue righteousness and that the Lord will gather his remnant together like a shepherd does his sheep.

TRUTH: What is the eternal truth that God is revealing to you?

____

____

____

____

____

APPLICATION: How will you apply this truth to your life?

____

____

____

____

____

PRAYER: Ask God to help you to live out this truth.

____

____

____

____

____

DAY 20

MICAH 3

Context

Chapter 3 opens with Micah condemning the corruption of the leaders and prophets, comparing the leadership to butchers who mutilate the people of God and the prophets as those who mislead the people with cries of peace. Micah warns them that their perversion and treachery won't go unpunished and reminds us that the role of spiritual leadership is one of humble and God-honoring service not a platform for personal gain.

TRUTH: What is the eternal truth that God is revealing to you?

____

____

____

____

____

APPLICATION: How will you apply this truth to your life?

____

____

____

____

PRAYER: Ask God to help you to live out this truth.

____

____

____

____

DAY 21

Sabbath Day

Today marks a Rest Day. The focus is simple: rest in the presence of God. Whether it's an opportunity to catch up on the reading plan, journal reflections on your spiritual journey, or engage in concentrated prayer, the key is to spend meaningful time in God's presence. Take this day to reconnect, absorb the lessons learned, and prioritize a moment of restful communion with God.

Reflect and write about what God has taught you this past week.

DAY 22
MICAH 4

Context

In chapter 4 Micah prophesies of a new era of peace that will come in the last days. Like a lighthouse, God's house will be set upon the highest point and will become the main attraction and source of wisdom for all the nations. Peace, tranquility, and contentment will be the order of the day and those who had been afflicted will be restored. However, before this can happen there must be suffering before redemption. Even with prophesies of peace Israel must first experience exile in Babylon.

TRUTH: What is the eternal truth that God is revealing to you?

____

____

____

____

____

APPLICATION: How will you apply this truth to your life?

____

____

____

____

____

PRAYER: Ask God to help you to live out this truth.

____

____

____

____

____

MICAH 5

Context

This prophetically significant chapter shines bright amidst the pages of the Old Testament giving us a glimpse into God's redemptive plan. A ruler, born in Bethlehem will bring deliverance to his people. This chapter also covers God's plan to purge the land of idolatry and warfare bringing an end to Israel's enemies.

TRUTH: What is the eternal truth that God is revealing to you?

____

____

____

____

____

APPLICATION: How will you apply this truth to your life?

____

____

____

____

____

PRAYER: Ask God to help you to live out this truth.

____

____

____

____

____

DAY 24

MICAH 6

Context

Chapter 6 opens with an indictment from the Lord against Israel, reminding them of his faithfulness in freeing them from slavery and giving them Godly leadership in Moses, Aaron, and Miriam. Through Micah, He defines that true worship is not in extravagant sacrifices but in offerings of justice, kindness, and humility. He closes this chapter with consequences for their unjust business practices and promises punishments similar to what they experienced in Egypt.

TRUTH: What is the eternal truth that God is revealing to you?

____

____

____

____

____

APPLICATION: How will you apply this truth to your life?

____

____

____

____

PRAYER: Ask God to help you to live out this truth.

____

____

____

____

____

DAY 25
MICAH 7:1-13

Context

Israel, God's chosen people have strayed away from his commands, and like a cancer moral corruption has metastasized into every aspect of society. However, regardless of the immesuarable despair and impending destruction, the prophet continues to have unwavering faith in the faithfulness of God.

TRUTH: What is the eternal truth that God is revealing to you?

____

____

____

____

____

APPLICATION: How will you apply this truth to your life?

____

____

____

____

____

PRAYER: Ask God to help you to live out this truth.

____

____

____

____

____

DAY 26

MICAH 7:14-20

Context

Micah implores the Lord to shepherd this flock of lost sheep again while meditating on the great miracles and promises in the hope that God will show his kindness again. He concludes this chapter with an encouraging message of redemption, mercy, and compassion, declaring that the sins of the people will be buried in a watery grave.

TRUTH: What is the eternal truth that God is revealing to you?

____

____

____

____

____

APPLICATION: How will you apply this truth to your life?

____

____

____

____

____

PRAYER: Ask God to help you to live out this truth.

____

____

____

____

OVERVIEW - JONAH

Jonah was not a fan of the assignment the LORD gave him. His grievance was rooted in his opinion of those he was to speak to and what he felt they deserved. For Jonah, the people of Nineveh were not worthy of hearing from God considering their sin and wretchedness.

While Jonah is on a mission to deliver a message, his heart becomes the message for the believer reading this book today. He was reluctant to share God's word with people he did not think would receive it. This book highlights that, like Jonah, believers ought not to determine in their heart who is worthy of being preached to, especially when the LORD commands otherwise. This book is a reminder that "all have sinned and fallen short of the glory of God" (Romans 3:23). Our hope for those who are far from God should be that they repent and return to Him with sincerity.

DAY 27

JONAH 1

Context

In chapter 1 the prophet Jonah shows us the fruitless result of attempting to flee from the instruction of the Lord. His rebellion led to the misfortune of others, being thrown overboard and eventually being swallowed by a great fish. His refusal to deliver the word of the Lord to a wicked city triggered a series of events designed to change his heart.

TRUTH: What is the eternal truth that God is revealing to you?

____

____

____

____

____

APPLICATION: How will you apply this truth to your life?

____

____

____

____

____

PRAYER: Ask God to help you to live out this truth.

____

____

____

____

____

DAY 28

Sabbath Day

Today marks a Rest Day. The focus is simple: rest in the presence of God. Whether it's an opportunity to catch up on the reading plan, journal reflections on your spiritual journey, or engage in concentrated prayer, the key is to spend meaningful time in God's presence. Take this day to reconnect, absorb the lessons learned, and prioritize a moment of restful communion with God.

Reflect and write about what God has taught you this past week.

DAY 29

JONAH 2

Context

Trapped in the belly of a great fish deep beneath the surface Jonah calls out to the Lord in great distress knowing that his God was the source of his deliverance. His prayer of repentance ends with the declaration that those who pay regard to worthless idols forsake the steadfast love of God. After this, the Lord spoke to the great fish and commanded it to spit Jonah out on dry land.

TRUTH: What is the eternal truth that God is revealing to you?

____

____

____

____

____

APPLICATION: How will you apply this truth to your life?

____

____

____

____

____

PRAYER: Ask God to help you to live out this truth.

____

____

____

____

____

DAY 30

Context

Jonah 3 shows us the willingness of God to give us second chances even when we are reluctant to follow his instructions. Jonah obeys and proclaims the message of imminent destruction in forty days. The people of Nineveh call for a city-wide repentance with fasting, sack cloths, and ashes even relegating their animals to strict adherence. The Lord sees their repentance and humility and shows them mercy.

TRUTH: What is the eternal truth that God is revealing to you?

____

____

____

____

____

APPLICATION: How will you apply this truth to your life?

____

____

____

____

____

PRAYER: Ask God to help you to live out this truth.

____

____

____

____

____

DAY 31

JONAH 4

Context

The final chapter of the book ends with the prophet being displeased with the Lord's decision to spare the people of Nineveh. He explains that he knew that the Lord was gracious, merciful, and slow to anger, and that because of these qualities that is why he fled. Sulking under a makeshift structure and demanding death, the Lord through an example of a plant that he caused to grow and die showed the prophet the value of human life.

TRUTH: What is the eternal truth that God is revealing to you?

____

____

____

____

____

APPLICATION: How will you apply this truth to your life?

____

____

____

____

____

PRAYER: Ask God to help you to live out this truth.

____

____

____

____

____

9 798218 451110